I WANT TO KNOW

Was Atlantis Real?

Portia Summers

Enslow Publishing
101 W. 23rd Street
Suite 240
New York, NY 10011
USA

enslow.com

Published in 2018 by Enslow Publishing, LLC.
101 W. 23rd Street, Suite 240, New York, NY 10011

Library of Congress Cataloging-in-Publication Data

Names: Summers, Portia, author.
Title: Was Atlantis real? / Portia Summers.
Description: New York, NY : Enslow Publishing, 2018. | Series: I want to know | Audience: Grades 3 to 5. | Includes bibliographical references and index.
Identifiers: LCCN 2017010003| ISBN 9780766092013 (library bound) | ISBN 9780766093782 (paperback) | ISBN 9780766093799 (6 pack)
Subjects: LCSH: Atlantis (Legendary place)—Juvenile literature.
Classification: LCC GN751 .S89 2018 | DDC 001.94—dc23
LC record available at https://lccn.loc.gov/2017010003

Printed in China

To Our Readers: We have done our best to make sure all websites in this book were active and appropriate when we went to press. However, the author and the publisher have no control over and assume no liability for the material available on those websites or on any websites they may link to. Any comments or suggestions can be sent by email to customerservice@enslow.com.

Photo Credits: Cover diversepixel/Shutterstock.com ; pp. 3, 7 Vuk Kostic/Shutterstock.com; pp. 5, 6 Print Collector/Hulton Archive/Getty Images; p. 11 Katie May/Shutterstock.com; pp. 13, 23 © Look and Learn/Bridgeman Images; p. 15 Heritage Images/Hulton Archive/Getty Images; p. 16 Laszlo Halasi/Shutterstock.com; p. 19 Imagno/Hulton Archive/Getty Images; p. 20 jgorzynik/Shutterstock.com; p. 25 Historical Picture Archive/Corbis Historical/Getty Images; p. 26 Crystal Eye Studio/Shutterstock.com; p. 27 dieKleinert/Alamy Stock Photo.

Contents

Chapter 1

. . . .

A City Beneath the Sea

Legend tells of an island city that was peaceful, profitable, and beautiful. The dwellers of this island were happy and healthy. But they became greedy and started a war with a nation on land. The gods became angry with the citizens of this island and drowned it. The name of this city was Atlantis.

Plato's Story

In ancient Greece, there was a **philosopher** and teacher named Plato (c. 428–c. 348 BCE). Plato helped found one of the world's first universities, the University of Athens. He taught thinkers, politicians, and even royalty. He was

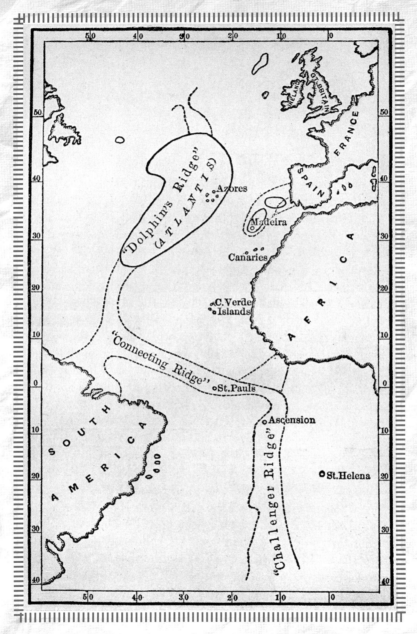

This map from 1882 shows one of the many places historians thought Atlantis could have been located. In this version, it is somewhere in the North Atlantic Ocean.

well known in his lifetime for being one of the smartest and most knowledgeable men alive. He didn't just give lectures, however. Plato also wrote down his thoughts and lessons, which gives many historians today a glimpse at the way ancient Greeks thought.

In some of his most famous works, *Timaeus* and *Criteas* (written around 360 BCE), Plato wrote about an island city that had been swallowed by the ocean. The island was supposed to be larger than Asia Minor (Turkey and Persia) and ancient Libya combined and was a mountainous region with a large flat plain in its center.

Plato, the famous Greek philosopher, was one of the first people to write down stories of Atlantis.

Home to Demigods and Man

According to Plato, the god of the sea, Poseidon, fell in love with a **mortal** woman, Cleito, who gave birth to five sets of male twins. The oldest of these was Atlas, who was made king of the island city. Poseidon created the island for his

Imagine That!

The Atlantic Ocean was named after Atlas, son of Poseidon, and the fabled city of Atlantis.

According to legend, the god of the sea, Poseidon, created Atlantis for his family.

family to live on. Many people from around the known world came to live there with the family and created a peaceful, prosperous society.

The city was built into the mountains of the island, surrounded by moats and rivers. Every entrance to the city was heavily guarded, and its citizens enjoyed safety, wealth, and happiness. The island was said to be filled with natural resources such as precious metals. Its people were known for building great ships and being great sailors. Life in Atlantis was paradise.

The Greek Gods

In ancient Greece, the people worshipped many gods. Each god controlled one aspect of life, from the weather to war and even love. Here are a few of the main gods of ancient Greece (later adopted by the ancient Romans):

Zeus (Jupiter): King of the gods and ruler of Mount Olympus, where the gods lived; god of lightning, thunder, and justice.

Hera (Juno): Queen of the gods; goddess of marriage and family.

Poseidon (Neptune): brother of Zeus and god of the ocean.

But despite all of this, the people of Atlantis became greedy and decided to go to war. And this, according to legend, was the **downfall** of Atlantis.

Hades (Orcus): brother of Zeus and god of the underworld.

Demeter (Ceres): sister of Zeus and the goddess of fertility, the seasons, and agriculture.

Athena (Minerva): daughter of Zeus and the goddess of wisdom, literature, science, and strategic warfare.

Artemis (Diana): daughter of Zeus and twin sister to Apollo; goddess of the hunt, archery, and the moon.

Apollo: son of Zeus and twin brother of Artemis; god of light, prophecy, inspiration, poetry, music, and medicine.

Ares (Mars): son of Zeus and Hera; god of war and violence.

Aphrodite (Venus): goddess of love and beauty.

Hermes (Mercury): son of Zeus, the messenger of the gods; god of communication, eloquence, thieves, and games.

Hephastus (Vulcan): son of Hera and Zeus, god of fire and blacksmiths.

Hestia (Vesta): sister of Zeus, goddess of the hearth and the home.

Dionysus (Bacchus): god of wine, parties, and the theater.

Eros (Cupid): son of Aphrodite and Ares, god of love and beauty.

Persephone (Proserpina): wife of Hades, goddess of spring.

Chapter 2

. . . .

The Legend of Atlantis

Atlantis was said to be a **utopia** where all its citizens were happy. They all lived in beautiful houses, had plenty to eat, and despite the many types of people that lived on the island, lived in peace with each other. But as is so often the case, the people of Atlantis weren't satisfied with this. They wanted more.

So the Atlanteans went to war with neighboring cities on land. They conquered parts of Libya, sections of the land across the Strait of Gibraltar and the Pillars of Hercules, and as far away as Tyrrhenia (modern-day Italy). They enslaved the people they conquered, forcing them to work without pay and to help the city of Atlantis against their will.

The Strait of Gibraltar in Spain is one of the many areas that the Atlanteans were said to have conquered.

Angry Gods

This angered the gods, who felt that the Atlanteans had been so blessed and favored that wanting more was selfish. So they caused earthquakes and floods that sent the island of Atlantis and all its inhabitants into the ocean.

According to the ancient Greeks, the sea where Atlantis once stood became impassable for all ships, which explained parts of the Atlantic Ocean that were very rough and filled with rocks.

This twentieth-century painting shows the destruction of Atlantis.

Real Life?

Many historians think that Plato's story was inspired after he visited the island of Sicily, off the coast of Italy. Others think that Plato and his students perhaps visited Egypt, where they heard stories and saw hieroglyphs that told of an island that had disappeared into the sea. Others theorized that some of the islands in the Mediterranean might have been the inspiration for Atlantis, including Sardinia, Crete, Santorini, Cyprus, and Malta. It has also been thought that the island was even farther away, perhaps in Norway or even Ireland.

It was also said that the druids in what is today the United Kingdom were survivors of Atlantis, since they had advanced knowledge about nature. The druids were a highly respected group among the ancient Celts. The druids served as spiritual leaders, judges, doctors, and teachers. However, they spread their knowledge **orally** and kept no written records. What is known of the druids comes from other cultures. So while the druids were

Because the druids were so knowledgeable of the earth, the stars, and the oceans, many people thought that they may have been the survivors of Atlantis.

mysterious, and some believe magical, it is much more likely that any druids that came from places other than England or Ireland probably came from Gaul (modern-day France), not Atlantis.

Chapter 3

· · · · · · · · · ·

Waves of Stories

Over the centuries, many philosophers and historians debated whether or not Atlantis really existed, or if it was simply a story meant to warn people. Even though the culture of ancient Greece fell, as did the Roman Empire after it, their stories and philosophies remained and spread throughout the world.

Fact or Fable?

Jewish and Christian thinkers also discussed Atlantis. Some seemed to think the island really did exist and that it was an entire civilization that had been wiped out by the wrath of God. Some thought it was destroyed in the biblical great flood that was survived by Noah and his ark. Others thought that the island was indeed real but had become abandoned as resources disappeared.

Flemish **cartographer** Abraham Ortelius was one of the first mapmakers to see that the continents seemed to have at one time been one large land mass called Pangea. According to Ortelius, it was possible that the island of Atlantis was formed as a series of earthquakes shook the continents apart and was destroyed in the same way.

Sir Thomas Moore wrote a now-famous work of fiction called *Utopia* in the sixteenth century. In it he described an idealistic culture inspired by the stories of Atlantis and by first-hand accounts of explorers traveling to the New World. One of the main characters even gives a description of the fabled lost city.

Imagine That!

The Atlanteans created a huge temple to the god Poseidon. On top of this temple was supposed to be a massive statue of the sea god made entirely of gold.

This medieval painting shows Noah's ark. Some historians thought that the story of Noah's ark involved Atlantis.

Survivors and Descendants

The Maya were a great civilization that lived in Central America between 2000 BCE and 1697 AD. They had a complex society much like the ancient Greeks. They built elaborate temples, practiced a religion where

This is the Temple of Kukulkan in the Mayan site Chichen Itza in Mexico. When European explorers discovered the advanced civilizations in Central and South America, they thought perhaps survivors of Atlantis had made it to the New World.

they worshipped many gods, created large cities, and cultivated crops.

In 1511, just a few years after Christopher Columbus first sailed to America and brought back news of the

New World to Europe, a Spanish ship was wrecked in the Caribbean. Afterward, the Spanish explorers made contact with the Maya. While many survivors of the shipwreck did not make it back to Europe, two managed to do so and told stories of these people with the complicated religion and **ornate** buildings. They even had their own calendar and form of writing.

Over the centuries, more explorers were sent to Central America, eventually nearly wiping out the Maya and their culture. The same happened to the culture of the Aztecs to the south, who had an equally **sophisticated** society.

Many Europeans at the time thought that **indigenous** people were inferior to Europeans and did not think that a culture as complex as that of the Maya could have developed on its own. Instead, they thought that the Mayan civilization was created by survivors from the city of Atlantis, who somehow made it to the New World. These survivors of Atlantis lived with the indigenous people and helped them create their

Atlantis in Books and Movies

Atlantis has inspired countless stories over the centuries. Here is short list of books and films that have been inspired by the legend:

20,000 Leagues Under the Sea, Jules Verne (novel, 1861)

The Maracot Deep, Arthur Conan Doyle (novel, 1927)

Neverwhere, Neil Gaiman (television series and novel, 1996)

The Magician's Nephew, C. S. Lewis (novel, 1955)

"*The Temple*," H. P. Lovecraft (short story, 1925)

Journey to the Center of the Earth (movie, 1959)

Atlantis: The Lost Continent (movie, 1961)

Atlantis: The Lost Empire (movie, 2001), and its sequel *Atlantis: Milo's Return* (2003)

Journey 2: The Mysterious Island (movie, 2012, sequel to 2008's *Journey to the Center of the Earth*)

complex religion, build their cities and temples, and develop their style of writing.

In 1882, American politician and writer Ignatious Donnelly went one step further in his book *Atlantis: The Antediluvian World*. In it, he said that all ancient societies were in fact **descended** from survivors of Atlantis. A few years later, Russian mystic Madame Blavatsky said that not only were Atlanteans the creators of all ancient civilization, but also the ancestors of the **Aryans,** an ancient people who spoke an Indo-European language and migrated to the Indian subcontinent in prehistoric times. She published a book that she claimed was actually written in Atlantis called *The Secret Doctrine*. Many of her followers believe that she was a direct descendent of the citizens of Atlantis, although neither of these was ever proven.

This French educational card shows an Aryan farmer and warrior. Some thought that the Aryans were descendants of the citizens of Atlantis. There was no science to back this claim, but that didn't stop many people from believing it.

Chapter 4

· · · · · · · · · · ·

Myth, Legend, or Possible?

Although many of the stories related to Atlantis have been proven incorrect, there are still archaeologists and historians who think the city might have once been real.

The Search Continues

In 2011, archaeologist Richard Freund, who led a team from the University of Hartford, claimed to have found evidence of Atlantis in southwestern Andalusia (in Spain). Other researchers have suggested that Atlantis was off the coast of Spain. Still others have thought that the mythical island of Atlantis was in fact a Caribbean island or even an island off the coast of Africa.

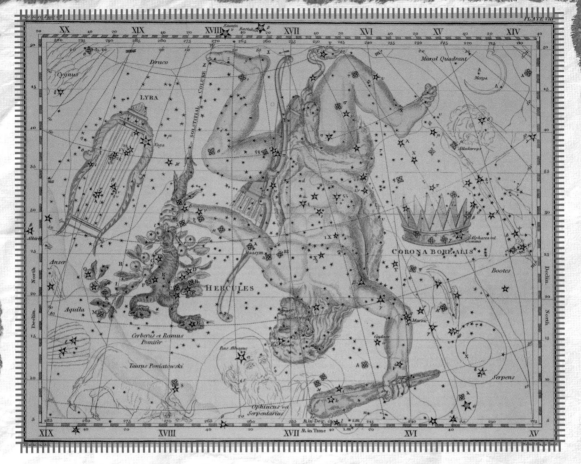

This illustration shows the constellations of Lyra, Hercules, and Corona. Lyra is named after the lyre, an ancient Greek harp.

Imagine That!

Some believed that because the people of Atlantis were so advanced, they must have been aliens. Supposedly, these people came from the star system Lyra and could live to be eight hundred years old!

Sunken Continents

Although the story of Atlantis has been considered a myth for many years, there is new research to suggest that, in fact, there are sunken islands and even continents.

In 2017 it was revealed that scientist Lewis Ashwal of the University of Witwatersrand in South Africa discovered the remains of a continent in the Indian Ocean between India and Madagascar. The continent is now scattered across the ocean floor. It sunk into the ocean as India and Madagascar split farther apart eighty-five million years ago. Pieces of the continent could be as far away as Australia and may even create the base for some of the volcanic islands in the Indian Ocean.

Another sunken continent, also revealed in 2017, is now mostly submerged beneath the South Pacific. Called Zealandia by scientists, it measures 1.9 million square miles (5 million square kilometers) and is 94 percent underwater. New Zealand is the part of this continental mass that is above water.

Could either of these be the lost city of Atlantis?

More Than a Story

Perhaps the most amazing thing about the tale of Atlantis is that the story continues to inspire others. Many writers, artists, and poets have found **inspiration** in the idea of Atlantis.

Although few scientists actually believe the legend of Atlantis is true, a few believe that it could have been based on true events. Ocean explorer Robert Ballard, who discovered the wreck of the *Titanic* in 1985, explains that

This painting shows the volcanic explosion that destroyed Santorini. Natural disasters have wiped out civilizations throughout history.

many **catastrophic** volcanoes and floods have occurred during human history. One such instance was on the island of Santorini in Greece. About 3,600 years ago, a massive volcanic eruption devastated the advanced society of Minoans that lived on the island. The civilization disappeared soon after.

Although scientists have yet to prove the existence of Atlantis, it is possible that the island country really existed. After all, the earth is constantly changing, and the ocean is far from conquered. There are thousands of miles along the ocean floor that have never been seen by humans. There may be a real lost city beneath the waves, waiting to be rediscovered.

Words to Know

Aryans An ancient people who migrated into the Indian subcontinent about 1500 BCE.

cartographer A mapmaker.

catastrophic Causing great damage.

descended To be a direct blood relative of someone from the past.

downfall A loss of power or status.

indigenous Native.

inspiration Something that causes a feeling or action.

mortal Human; having an end of life.

orally Spread by spoken language.

ornate Having many decorations.

philosopher A deep thinker who seeks wisdom and ponders questions about life and the universe.

sophisticated Highly complicated.

utopia A society that is considered perfect, where the people are peaceful and well taken care of.

Further Reading

Books

Hyde, Natalie. *The Lost City of Atlantis*. New York, NY: Crabtree Publishing, 2016.

Pearson, Anne. *DK Eyewitness Books: Ancient Greece*. Washington, DC: DK Children, 2014.

Rajczak, Kristen. *Did Atlantis Exist?* New York, NY: Gareth Stevens, 2015.

Rea, Amy C. *The Mystery of Atlantis*. Minneapolis, MN: Core Library, 2016.

Websites

Easy Science for Kids

easyscienceforkids.com/all-about-the-lost-city-of-atlantis/
Read more fun facts about the lost city of Atlantis.

History for Kids

www.historyforkids.net/ancient-greece.html
Learn more about life in ancient Greece, including its art, science, literature, and religion.

National Geographic

www.nationalgeographic.com/archaeology-and-history/ archaeology/atlantis/
Dive deeper into the legend of Atlantis by reading fascinating articles.

Index